**Title: The Ultimate Guide to Creating a Profitable Print-on-Demand Store with Etsy and Printify**

**Table of Contents:**

## Chapter 1: Introduction to Print-on-Demand and Etsy

Welcome to the world of print-on-demand (POD) and Etsy—a dynamic combination that has revolutionized the way artists, entrepreneurs, and creatives bring their visions to life and share them with the world.

### Understanding Print-on-Demand:

Print-on-demand is a business model where products are only produced once an order is received. This means that creators don't need to hold inventory or invest in bulk manufacturing upfront. Instead, they can upload their designs to a POD platform, and when a customer places an order, the product is printed and shipped directly to the buyer. This model offers several advantages, including:

1. **Low Overhead Costs:** Since creators don't need to invest in inventory or storage space, the overhead costs associated with running a print-on-demand business are significantly lower compared to traditional retail models.

2. **Flexibility and Scalability:** Print-on-demand allows creators to experiment with different designs and products without the risk of excess inventory. As demand grows, creators can easily scale their business by adding new designs or expanding their product offerings.

3. **Global Reach:** With print-on-demand, creators can reach customers around the world without the need

for international shipping or distribution networks. This opens up opportunities to tap into new markets and audiences.

**Exploring the Etsy Platform:**

Etsy is an online marketplace that specializes in handmade, vintage, and unique goods. Founded in 2005, Etsy has grown into a global community of independent sellers and creative entrepreneurs, offering a wide range of products across various categories, including art, jewelry, home decor, and more. Some key benefits of selling on Etsy include:

1. **Built-In Audience:** Etsy attracts millions of buyers who are looking for unique and handmade products. By selling on Etsy, creators can tap into this existing audience and gain exposure for their designs.

2. **Seller-Friendly Tools:** Etsy provides sellers with a suite of tools and resources to help them manage their shops effectively. From customizable storefronts to marketing and analytics tools, Etsy offers everything creators need to succeed.

3. **Community Support:** Etsy fosters a sense of community among its sellers, providing opportunities for networking, collaboration, and mentorship. Sellers can connect with other creators, share tips and advice, and learn from each other's experiences.

**Why Print-on-Demand and Etsy Make a Winning Combination:**

The combination of print-on-demand and Etsy offers a powerful platform for artists, designers, and entrepreneurs to turn their creative ideas into profitable businesses. By leveraging the benefits of print-on-demand—such as low overhead costs, flexibility, and scalability—alongside the built-in audience and seller-friendly tools of Etsy, creators can reach customers worldwide and build a thriving online business.

In the chapters that follow, we'll dive deeper into the world of print-on-demand and Etsy, exploring everything from setting up your shop and designing products to marketing your creations and scaling your business for success. Get ready to unleash your creativity and embark on an exciting journey of entrepreneurship in the digital age.

## Chapter 2: Understanding Printify: A Comprehensive Overview

Printify stands as a cornerstone in the realm of print-on-demand, offering a seamless platform for creators to bring their designs to life and share them with the world. In this chapter, we'll take a deep dive into Printify, exploring its features, functionalities, and the myriad benefits it provides to entrepreneurs and artists alike.

### What is Printify?

Printify is a leading print-on-demand platform that connects creators with a network of print providers worldwide. Founded in 2015, Printify has quickly become a go-to solution for individuals looking to launch their own custom merchandise businesses without the need for upfront investment or inventory management.

**Key Features of Printify:**

1. **Extensive Product Catalog:** Printify offers a vast selection of customizable products, ranging from apparel and accessories to home decor and stationery. Creators can choose from a wide variety of items to showcase their designs, including t-shirts, hoodies, mugs, tote bags, phone cases, and more.

2. **Supplier Integration:** Printify partners with a network of reputable print providers located in different regions around the world. This allows creators to select suppliers based on factors such as product quality, pricing, and shipping times, ensuring that they can deliver high-quality products to their customers efficiently.

3. **Easy-to-Use Design Tools:** Printify's design tools make it simple for creators to upload their artwork, customize product designs, and visualize how their designs will look on various items. With user-friendly interfaces and intuitive features, creators can bring their creative vision to life with ease.

4. **Seamless Integration with E-commerce Platforms:** Printify seamlessly integrates with popular e-commerce platforms like Shopify, WooCommerce, and Etsy. This integration allows creators to sync their Printify products with their online stores, manage

orders, and track inventory automatically, streamlining the process of running a print-on-demand business.

5. **Competitive Pricing Options:** Printify offers competitive pricing options for creators, allowing them to set their own profit margins and adjust prices to meet their business goals. With transparent pricing and no hidden fees, creators can confidently price their products while maximizing their profits.

6. **Quality Control and Fulfillment:** Printify's print providers adhere to strict quality control standards to ensure that each product meets the highest quality standards. From printing to packaging and shipping, Printify's fulfillment process is designed to provide a seamless and reliable experience for both creators and customers.

**Why Choose Printify?**

Printify offers a multitude of benefits for creators looking to start or expand their print-on-demand businesses:

- **Low Risk, High Reward:** With no upfront costs or inventory requirements, Printify offers a low-risk way for creators to launch their own custom merchandise businesses and generate passive income.

- **Scalability:** Printify's platform is designed to scale with creators as their businesses grow. Whether you're a solo entrepreneur or a seasoned business owner,

Printify offers the flexibility and scalability to meet your evolving needs.

- **Global Reach:** With print providers located around the world, Printify allows creators to reach customers globally and expand their customer base beyond geographical boundaries.

- **Support and Resources:** Printify provides creators with a wealth of support and resources to help them succeed. From educational guides and tutorials to responsive customer support, Printify is committed to empowering creators to achieve their goals.

In the following chapters, we'll explore how to integrate Printify with your chosen e-commerce platform, select the right products and suppliers, and optimize your print-on-demand business for success. With Printify as your partner, the possibilities for creating and selling custom products are endless.

### Chapter 3: Getting Started with Etsy: Setting Up Your Shop

Congratulations on taking the first step towards launching your print-on-demand business! In this chapter, we'll guide you through the process of setting up your Etsy shop, from creating an account to customizing your shop settings and uploading product listings. By the end of this chapter, you'll have a fully functional Etsy shop ready to showcase your print-on-demand products to the world.

### 1. Creating an Etsy Account:

The first step in setting up your Etsy shop is to create an Etsy account. Visit the Etsy website and click on the "Sign Up" button located at the top right corner of the page. Follow the prompts to create your account, including providing your email address, choosing a username and password, and agreeing to Etsy's terms of use.

## 2. Customizing Your Shop Settings:

Once you've created your Etsy account, it's time to customize your shop settings. Click on the "Sell on Etsy" link located in the top right corner of the page, then select "Open Your Etsy Shop." Follow the prompts to fill out information about your shop, including your shop name, language, currency, and location. You'll also have the option to upload a profile picture and banner image to personalize your shop's appearance.

## 3. Adding Your Shop Policies:

Next, you'll need to add your shop policies, including your shipping, payment, and return policies. These policies help set expectations for your customers and provide them with important information about how transactions will be handled. You can access your shop policies by clicking on the "Settings" tab in your Etsy dashboard and selecting "Info & Appearance" from the dropdown menu.

## 4. Uploading Product Listings:

With your shop settings in place, it's time to start uploading product listings. Click on the "Listings" tab in your Etsy dashboard and select "Add a listing." Fill out the details for each product listing, including the title, description, price, quantity, and shipping options. Be sure to upload high-quality photos of your products to showcase them effectively to potential customers.

## 5. Optimizing Your Product Listings:

To attract potential customers to your Etsy shop, it's essential to optimize your product listings for search. Use relevant keywords and tags in your product titles and descriptions to improve your visibility in Etsy's search results. You can also take advantage of Etsy's built-in SEO tools to help optimize your listings for search.

## 6. Promoting Your Etsy Shop:

Once your Etsy shop is up and running, it's time to start promoting it to attract customers. Share your shop and product listings on social media platforms, create engaging content to showcase your products, and consider running promotions or discounts to incentivize purchases. Building an online presence and engaging with your audience will help drive traffic to your Etsy shop and increase sales.

## Conclusion:

Setting up your Etsy shop is the first step towards building a successful print-on-demand business. By creating a professional and inviting shop, optimizing your product listings for search, and promoting your shop to attract customers, you'll be well on your way to achieving success on Etsy. In the next chapter, we'll explore strategies for selecting profitable niches and designing products that resonate with your target audience.

## Chapter 4: Selecting Profitable Niches for Your Print-on-Demand Store

Selecting the right niche is a critical step in building a successful print-on-demand business. In this chapter, we'll delve into the importance of niche selection and provide strategies for identifying profitable niches with high demand and low competition. By the end of this chapter, you'll have the tools and insights needed to choose a niche that aligns with your interests, attracts your target audience, and maximizes your chances of success.

### Understanding the Importance of Niche Selection:

In the crowded marketplace of print-on-demand, standing out from the competition is essential to success. By focusing on a specific niche, you can differentiate your store and appeal to a targeted audience with specific interests and needs. Niche selection allows you to position yourself as an expert in your chosen area and build a loyal customer base that values your unique offerings.

### Strategies for Identifying Profitable Niches:

1. **Research Market Trends:** Start by researching market trends and identifying emerging niches with high demand. Look for industries or topics that are experiencing growth or gaining traction, such as sustainable living, wellness, or niche hobbies. Keep an

eye on industry publications, social media trends, and online forums to stay informed about market developments

2. **Assess Competition:** Evaluate the level of competition within potential niches to determine their viability. Look for niches with moderate to low competition, where you can carve out a unique position and differentiate yourself from competitors. Avoid overly saturated niches where it may be challenging to stand out and attract customers.

3. **Consider Audience Needs:** Think about the needs and preferences of your target audience when selecting a niche. Consider demographic factors such as age, gender, location, and interests to identify niche markets with a built-in audience that aligns with your products. Conduct surveys or engage with potential customers to gather insights into their preferences and pain points.

4. **Follow Your Passions:** Choose a niche that aligns with your interests, passions, and expertise. Building a print-on-demand business around a topic or hobby that you're passionate about will not only make the work more enjoyable but also increase your motivation and dedication to success. Your enthusiasm for the niche will shine through in your products and resonate with your audience.

**Tips for Researching Market Trends and Consumer Preferences:**

1. **Use Keyword Research Tools:** Utilize keyword research tools such as Google Trends, SEMrush, or Keyword Planner to identify popular search terms and topics related to your potential niches. Look for keywords with high search volume and low competition to uncover niche opportunities.

2. **Explore Social Media Platforms:** Monitor social media platforms like Instagram, Pinterest, and TikTok to gauge interest and engagement around specific niches. Pay attention to hashtags, trending topics, and popular accounts within your niche to identify opportunities for product creation and promotion.

3. **Join Online Communities:** Participate in online communities, forums, and Facebook groups related to your potential niches. Engage with members, ask questions, and observe discussions to gain insights into consumer preferences, pain points, and emerging trends within the niche.

4. **Analyze Competitor Strategies:** Study your competitors' product offerings, pricing strategies, and marketing tactics to identify gaps and opportunities within your chosen niche. Look for ways to differentiate your products and offer unique value to customers that competitors may be overlooking.

**Conclusion:**

Selecting a profitable niche is a foundational step in building a successful print-on-demand store. By conducting thorough research, assessing competition, considering audience needs, and following your passions, you can identify niche markets with high demand and low competition. In the next chapter, we'll explore strategies for designing products that resonate with your target audience and set your store apart from the competition.

### Chapter 5: Designing Your Products: Tips for Success

Designing captivating and marketable products is crucial for the success of your print-on-demand business. In this chapter, we'll delve into essential product design strategies, share best practices for creating eye-catching designs, and offer tips for staying inspired and relevant in a competitive market. By the end of this chapter, you'll be equipped with the knowledge and skills needed to create products that resonate with your target audience and drive sales.

### Understanding the Importance of Product Design:

Product design plays a significant role in attracting customers, setting your brand apart, and driving sales in the print-on-demand industry. A well-designed product not only catches the eye but also communicates your brand's identity, values, and personality. By investing time and effort into thoughtful and creative design, you can create products that stand out from the competition and resonate with your target audience.

### Best Practices for Product Design:

1. **Know Your Audience:** Before diving into product design, take the time to understand your target audience's preferences, interests, and needs. Consider factors such as age, gender, lifestyle, and aesthetic preferences to tailor your designs to resonate with your audience effectively.

2. **Focus on Quality:** Quality is paramount when it comes to product design. Ensure that your designs are high-resolution, well-executed, and visually appealing. Pay attention to details such as color accuracy, typography, and composition to create professional-looking products that instill confidence in your customers.

3. **Keep It Simple:** When it comes to design, less is often more. Aim for clean, minimalist designs that convey your message clearly and effectively. Avoid cluttered or overly complicated designs that can overwhelm viewers and detract from the overall aesthetic appeal of your products.

4. **Stay On-Trend:** Keep abreast of design trends and incorporate them into your products where relevant. Follow industry publications, attend design conferences, and explore online resources to stay informed about emerging trends in typography, color palettes, and graphic styles. However, be mindful of trends that may quickly become outdated and focus on timeless design elements that have lasting appeal.

5. **Tell a Story:** Use your designs to tell a compelling story or evoke an emotional response from your audience. Consider incorporating storytelling elements, symbolism, or cultural references into your designs to create deeper connections with your customers and make your products more memorable.

**Tips for Sourcing Inspiration:**

1. **Explore Diverse Sources:** Draw inspiration from a wide range of sources, including art, nature, fashion, pop culture, and current events. Explore museums, galleries, and exhibitions, browse design blogs and websites, and immerse yourself in different cultural influences to spark creativity and generate fresh ideas.

2. **Keep a Design Journal:** Keep a design journal or sketchbook to jot down ideas, sketches, and inspirations as they come to you. Capture fleeting moments of inspiration and revisit them later when brainstorming new designs or projects.

3. **Collaborate and Seek Feedback:** Collaborate with fellow designers, artists, and creatives to exchange ideas, share feedback, and gain fresh perspectives on your work. Participate in design communities, join critique groups, and seek feedback from friends, family, and mentors to refine your designs and improve your skills.

4. **Experiment and Iterate:** Don't be afraid to experiment with different techniques, styles, and mediums in your design process. Embrace failure as a learning opportunity and iterate on your designs until you achieve the desired result. Allow yourself the freedom to explore new ideas and take creative risks in pursuit of innovation and growth.

**Conclusion:**

Effective product design is a cornerstone of success in the print-on-demand industry. By following best practices, staying informed about design trends, and sourcing inspiration from diverse sources, you can create products that resonate with your target audience and drive sales. In the next chapter, we'll explore how to integrate Printify with your Etsy shop and bring your designs to life through print-on-demand fulfillment.

## Chapter 6: Integrating Printify with Your Etsy Shop

Integrating Printify with your Etsy shop is a crucial step in streamlining your print-on-demand business operations and bringing your designs to life. In this chapter, we'll guide you through the process of connecting Printify to Etsy, importing product listings, and managing orders seamlessly. By the end of this chapter, you'll be ready to leverage Printify's integration with Etsy to scale your print-on-demand business and maximize efficiency.

### 1. Connecting Printify to Your Etsy Shop:

- Log in to your Printify account and navigate to the "Stores" tab.
- Click on "Add new store" and select "Etsy" from the list of available integrations.
- Follow the prompts to connect your Printify account to your Etsy shop. You'll need to grant permission for Printify to access your Etsy account.
- Once connected, you'll see your Etsy shop listed under the "Stores" tab in your Printify dashboard.

### 2. Importing Product Listings from Printify to Etsy:

- In your Printify dashboard, navigate to the "Stores" tab and select your Etsy shop.

- Click on "Add product" to browse Printify's catalog of customizable products.
- Choose the product you'd like to add to your Etsy shop and customize it with your design.
- Once you're satisfied with the design, click on "Publish" to publish the product to your Etsy shop.
- Fill out the product details, including title, description, price, and tags, to optimize your listing for search.

## 3. Managing Orders and Fulfillment:

- When a customer places an order for a product from your Etsy shop, Printify will automatically receive the order details.
- Log in to your Printify dashboard to view and manage your orders. You'll see all incoming orders from your Etsy shop listed under the "Orders" tab.
- Select the order you'd like to fulfill and choose the appropriate print provider from the list of available options.
- Customize the order details, such as shipping options and production preferences, to meet your customer's needs.
- Once the order is ready, the print provider will fulfill and ship the product directly to your customer, and the tracking information will be automatically updated in your Printify dashboard.

## 4. Optimizing Your Printify Settings:

- Take advantage of Printify's advanced settings to customize your fulfillment process and optimize your workflow.
- Set up production regions to ensure that orders are fulfilled by print providers located closest to your customers, minimizing shipping times and costs.
- Configure shipping settings, pricing rules, and production preferences to streamline your fulfillment process and maximize efficiency.

**Conclusion:**

Integrating Printify with your Etsy shop is a powerful way to streamline your print-on-demand business operations and bring your designs to life with ease. By following the step-by-step instructions outlined in this chapter, you'll be able to seamlessly connect Printify to your Etsy shop, import product listings, manage orders efficiently, and optimize your workflow for success. In the next chapter, we'll explore strategies for choosing the right products and suppliers on Printify to maximize the quality and profitability of your print-on-demand offerings.

**Chapter 7: Choosing the Right Products and Suppliers on Printify**

Selecting the right products and suppliers is crucial for the success of your print-on-demand business. In this chapter, we'll explore the diverse range of products available through Printify and provide tips for choosing reliable and high-quality suppliers. By the end of this chapter, you'll be equipped with the knowledge and tools needed to evaluate suppliers effectively and offer top-notch products to your customers.

## 1. Exploring Printify's Product Catalog:

Printify offers a vast selection of customizable products, ranging from apparel and accessories to home decor and stationery. Some of the popular product categories available on Printify include:

- Apparel: T-shirts, hoodies, tank tops, sweatshirts, and more.
- Accessories: Tote bags, hats, phone cases, and socks.
- Home Decor: Posters, canvas prints, mugs, pillows, and blankets.
- Stationery: Notebooks, greeting cards, stickers, and calendars.

Take the time to explore Printify's product catalog and identify which products align with your brand and target audience. Consider factors such as product popularity, demand, and profit margins when selecting products to offer in your store.

## 2. Evaluating Suppliers:

When choosing suppliers on Printify, it's essential to evaluate them based on factors such as product quality, pricing, and shipping times. Here are some tips for evaluating suppliers effectively:

- **Product Quality:** Look for suppliers with a track record of producing high-quality products. Check customer reviews and ratings to gauge the quality of the products offered by each supplier. Consider ordering samples to assess the quality firsthand before committing to a supplier.

- **Pricing:** Compare pricing across different suppliers to ensure that you're getting competitive rates. Keep in mind that pricing may vary depending on factors such as product type, printing method, and order quantity. Balance cost with quality to find the best value for your money.

- **Shipping Times:** Consider shipping times when choosing suppliers to ensure timely delivery to your customers. Look for suppliers with fast turnaround times and reliable shipping methods. Keep in mind that shipping times may vary depending on the supplier's location and production capacity.

- **Customer Service:** Pay attention to the level of customer service provided by each supplier. Choose suppliers that are responsive to inquiries, address concerns promptly, and provide excellent support throughout the order fulfillment process.

### 3. Building Relationships with Suppliers:

Building strong relationships with your suppliers is key to long-term success in the print-on-demand business. Communicate openly with your suppliers, provide feedback on product quality and performance, and maintain a professional and collaborative relationship. By fostering positive relationships with your suppliers, you can ensure a smooth and reliable supply chain and deliver exceptional products to your customers consistently.

**Conclusion:**

Choosing the right products and suppliers is essential for the success of your print-on-demand business. By exploring Printify's diverse product catalog, evaluating suppliers based on factors such as product quality, pricing, and shipping times, and building relationships with your suppliers, you can offer top-notch products to your customers and build a reputation for excellence in the marketplace. In the next chapter, we'll explore pricing strategies for your print-on-demand products to maximize profitability while remaining competitive in the market.

## Chapter 8: Pricing Strategies for Your Print-on-Demand Products

Pricing your print-on-demand products effectively is essential for balancing profitability with competitiveness in the market. In this chapter, we'll delve into various pricing strategies and models, offering insights into how to set prices that maximize profitability while remaining attractive to customers. By the end of this chapter, you'll be equipped with the knowledge and tools needed to implement effective pricing strategies for your print-on-demand products.

### 1. Understanding Pricing Models:

**a. Cost-Based Pricing:** This approach involves calculating the total cost of producing each product, including materials, labor, and overhead expenses, and adding a markup to determine the selling price. Cost-based pricing ensures that you cover your production costs while generating a profit margin.

**b. Competitor-Based Pricing:** Competitor-based pricing involves researching competitors' prices for similar products and setting your prices accordingly. This approach allows you to remain competitive in the market while benchmarking against existing offerings.

**c. Value-Based Pricing:** Value-based pricing focuses on the perceived value of your products to customers rather than production costs or competitors' prices. By emphasizing the unique value proposition of your products, you can justify higher prices and attract customers willing to pay for quality and exclusivity.

**2. Factors to Consider When Pricing Your Products:**

**a. Production Costs:** Consider the total cost of producing each product, including materials, printing fees, labor, and overhead expenses. Ensure that your selling price covers these costs while providing a reasonable profit margin.

**b. Market Demand:** Evaluate market demand for your products and adjust your prices accordingly. Consider factors such as customer preferences, trends, and seasonal variations in demand when setting prices.

**c. Perceived Value:** Assess the perceived value of your products to customers and price them accordingly. Highlight unique features, quality craftsmanship, and exclusive designs to justify higher prices and differentiate your products from competitors.

**d. Competitor Pricing:** Research competitors' prices for similar products and analyze pricing trends in the market. Set your prices competitively to attract customers while maintaining profitability.

### 3. Strategies for Setting Competitive Prices:

**a. Tiered Pricing:** Offer multiple pricing tiers for your products to appeal to different customer segments. Provide options for budget-conscious customers as well as premium offerings with additional features or customization options.

**b. Bundle Pricing:** Bundle related products together and offer them at a discounted price compared to purchasing items individually. Bundle pricing encourages customers to purchase multiple items and increases the average order value.

**c. Promotional Pricing:** Run limited-time promotions, discounts, or sales to incentivize purchases and attract new customers. Use promotional pricing strategically to create urgency and drive sales during peak shopping periods.

**d. Dynamic Pricing:** Monitor market conditions, demand fluctuations, and competitor pricing in real-time and adjust your prices accordingly. Implement dynamic pricing strategies to optimize revenue and remain competitive in the market.

**Conclusion:**

Pricing your print-on-demand products effectively requires careful consideration of production costs, market demand, and competitive factors. By implementing strategic pricing models and considering factors such as production costs, market demand, perceived value, and competitor pricing, you can set prices that maximize profitability while attracting customers and driving sales. In the next chapter, we'll explore marketing strategies for promoting your print-on-demand products and reaching your target audience effectively.

### Chapter 9: Optimizing Your Etsy Shop for Sales

Turning your Etsy shop into a sales powerhouse requires more than just listing products—it requires strategic optimization. In this chapter, we'll explore key tactics for maximizing sales and conversions on Etsy. By implementing these best practices, you'll create a compelling shopping experience that attracts customers and drives sales.

### 1. Crafting Compelling Product Listings:

- **Title Optimization:** Create descriptive and keyword-rich titles that accurately convey what your product is and its key features. Include relevant keywords that potential customers might use when searching for products like yours.

- **Engaging Descriptions:** Write detailed and engaging product descriptions that highlight the unique features and benefits of your products. Use storytelling techniques to evoke emotion and create a connection with potential buyers.
- **Clear and Concise Information:** Provide essential information such as product dimensions, materials, and care instructions. Make it easy for customers to understand what they're buying and what to expect.

## 2. Enhancing Product Photos:

- **High-Quality Images:** Use high-resolution images that showcase your products in the best possible light. Invest in professional photography or learn how to take high-quality photos yourself.
- **Multiple Angles and Close-Ups:** Include multiple photos that show different angles and details of your products. This helps customers get a better sense of what your products look like in real life.
- **Lifestyle Shots:** Incorporate lifestyle shots that demonstrate how your products can be used or styled. Show your products in context to help potential buyers visualize themselves using or wearing them.

## 3. Utilizing Keywords and Tags:

- **Keyword Research:** Conduct keyword research to identify relevant terms and phrases that potential customers might use to find products like yours. Use tools like Google Keyword Planner or Etsy's search bar to discover popular keywords in your niche.

- **Strategic Tagging:** Use all available tags to maximize your products' visibility in Etsy search results. Include both broad and specific tags that accurately describe your products and target potential buyers.

## 4. Optimizing Shop Policies and About Section:

- **Clear Shop Policies:** Clearly outline your shop policies regarding shipping, returns, and exchanges. Transparency builds trust with customers and reduces the likelihood of misunderstandings or disputes.
- **Compelling About Section:** Use your About section to tell your brand story and connect with potential customers on a personal level. Share your inspiration, values, and passion for your craft to create a memorable impression.

## 5. Providing Excellent Customer Service:

- **Prompt Responses:** Respond to customer inquiries and messages promptly and professionally. Prompt communication builds trust and demonstrates your commitment to customer satisfaction.
- **Fast Shipping:** Ship orders promptly and provide accurate tracking information to keep customers informed about the status of their orders. Fast and reliable shipping enhances the overall shopping experience and encourages repeat business.

## Conclusion:

Optimizing your Etsy shop for maximum sales requires attention to detail and a customer-centric approach. By crafting compelling product listings, enhancing product photos, utilizing keywords and tags effectively, and providing excellent customer service, you'll create an enticing shopping experience that attracts customers and drives sales. In the next chapter, we'll explore strategies for marketing your Etsy shop and reaching a wider audience of potential buyers.

**Chapter 10: Marketing Your Print-on-Demand Products on Etsy**

Marketing your print-on-demand products effectively on Etsy is crucial for attracting customers and driving sales. In this chapter, we'll explore various marketing strategies and techniques to help you promote your products and increase visibility on the Etsy platform.

## 1. Optimize Your Product Listings:

- Use descriptive titles that include relevant keywords to improve search visibility.
- Write compelling product descriptions that highlight key features and benefits.
- Utilize all available tags to maximize searchability and reach a broader audience.

## 2. Showcase Your Products with High-Quality Photos:

- Invest in professional product photography to showcase your products in the best possible light.
- Use multiple, high-resolution images that showcase different angles and details of your products.
- Incorporate lifestyle shots to help potential buyers visualize how your products can be used or styled.

### 3. Leverage Etsy's Promotional Tools:

- Participate in Etsy promotions such as sales events, holiday promotions, and discounts to attract customers.
- Utilize Etsy Ads to increase visibility by promoting your listings across the platform.
- Offer free shipping or discounts for bulk orders to incentivize purchases.

### 4. Engage with Your Audience:

- Respond promptly to customer inquiries and messages to build trust and credibility.
- Encourage customer reviews and feedback to establish social proof and improve your shop's reputation.
- Utilize Etsy's messaging and follow-up features to stay in touch with customers and nurture relationships.

### 5. Utilize Social Media and Content Marketing:

- Share your products on social media platforms such as Instagram, Facebook, and Pinterest to reach a broader audience.
- Create engaging content such as blog posts, videos, or tutorials related to your products to attract potential customers.
- Collaborate with influencers or bloggers in your niche to promote your products to their audience.

### 6. Offer Special Promotions and Discounts:

- Run limited-time promotions or flash sales to create urgency and encourage impulse purchases.
- Offer exclusive discounts or coupon codes to loyal customers or subscribers to incentivize repeat purchases.

- Create bundle deals or product packages to increase the average order value and encourage upsells.

## 7. Monitor and Analyze Your Results:

- Use Etsy's analytics tools to track the performance of your listings and identify areas for improvement.
- Monitor traffic sources, conversion rates, and sales data to understand what's working and adjust your marketing strategies accordingly.
- Test different marketing tactics and strategies to see which ones yield the best results and focus your efforts on those channels.

## Conclusion:

Marketing your print-on-demand products effectively on Etsy requires a combination of strategic optimization, promotion, and engagement. By optimizing your product listings, showcasing your products with high-quality photos, leveraging Etsy's promotional tools, engaging with your audience, utilizing socia media and content marketing, offering special promotions and discounts, and monitoring your results, you can attract more customers and drive sales on the Etsy platform. In the next chapter, we'll explore how to leverage SEO to drive traffic to your Etsy shop and increase visibility in search results.

## Chapter 11: Leveraging SEO to Drive Traffic to Your Etsy Shop

Search Engine Optimization (SEO) is a powerful tool for increasing visibility and driving traffic to your Etsy shop. In th s chapter, we'll explore how you can leverage SEO techniques to improve your shop's ranking in search engine results and attract more potential customers.

## 1. Keyword Research:

- Conduct thorough keyword research to identify relevant terms and phrases that potential customers are searching for.
- Use tools like Google Keyword Planner, Etsy's search bar, and third-party keyword research tools to discover popular keywords in your niche.
- Focus on long-tail keywords and phrases that are specific to your products and have lower competition.

## 2. Optimize Your Product Titles:

- Incorporate your target keywords naturally into your product titles to improve search visibility.
- Keep your titles descriptive, concise, and informative, while also including relevant keywords to attract both customers and search engines.
- Experiment with different variations of your titles to see which ones perform best in search results.

## 3. Write Compelling Product Descriptions:

- Use your target keywords strategically throughout your product descriptions to improve search visibility.
- Provide detailed and informative descriptions that highlight the key features, benefits, and uses of your products.
- Incorporate natural language and persuasive copywriting techniques to engage potential customers and encourage conversions.

## 4. Utilize Tags and Categories:

- Take advantage of Etsy's tagging system to further optimize your listings for search.
- Use all available tags to include relevant keywords and phrases that describe your products.

- Choose the most appropriate categories and subcategories for your products to ensure they appear in relevant search results.

## 5. Optimize Your Shop Policies and About Section:

- Include relevant keywords and phrases in your shop policies and about section to improve search visibility.
- Provide detailed information about your shop, including your brand story, inspiration, and values.
- Use natural language and avoid keyword stuffing to maintain a professional and authentic tone.

## 6. Encourage Reviews and Engagement:

- Encourage customers to leave reviews and feedback on your products to improve your shop's credibility and reputation.
- Respond promptly to customer inquiries and messages to build trust and establish a positive relationship with potential buyers.
- Engage with your audience through social media, blog posts, and email newsletters to drive traffic to your Etsy shop and increase visibility.

## 7. Monitor and Analyze Your Results:

- Use Etsy's analytics tools to track the performance of your listings and monitor changes in search visibility.
- Monitor your shop's traffic sources, conversion rates, and sales data to understand which SEO strategies are driving the most traffic and sales.
- Adjust your SEO strategy accordingly based on your findings and continue to experiment with different tactics to improve your shop's ranking in search results.

## Conclusion:

Leveraging SEO techniques is essential for driving traffic to your Etsy shop and increasing visibility in search engine results. By conducting keyword research, optimizing your product titles and descriptions, utilizing tags and categories, optimizing your shop policies and about section, encouraging reviews and engagement, and monitoring your results, you can improve your shop's ranking in search results and attract more potential customers. In the next chapter, we'll explore how to enhance your product listings with compelling descriptions to further engage potential buyers and drive conversions.

**Chapter 12: Enhancing Your Product Listings with Compelling Descriptions**

Crafting compelling product descriptions is essential for attracting potential buyers and driving conversions in your Etsy shop. In this chapter, we'll explore strategies for enhancing your product listings with persuasive and engaging descriptions that captivate customers and encourage them to make a purchase.

**1. Highlight Key Features and Benefits:**

- Start your product descriptions by highlighting the key features and benefits of your products.
- Focus on what sets your products apart from competitors and how they can solve a problem or fulfill a need for the customer.
- Use bullet points or short paragraphs to make the information easy to read and digest.

**2. Tell a Story:**

- Incorporate storytelling into your product descriptions to create an emotional connection with potential buyers.
- Share the inspiration behind your products, the story of how they were made, or the impact they can have on the customer's life.

- Use descriptive language and vivid imagery to paint a picture in the customer's mind and evoke their emotions.

## 3. Use Descriptive Language:

- Choose descriptive language that paints a clear picture of your products and their benefits.
- Use sensory words that appeal to the customer's senses, such as "soft," "luxurious," "vibrant," or "handcrafted."
- Avoid jargon or technical terms that may confuse or alienate potential buyers.

## 4. Provide Detailed Information:

- Provide detailed information about your products, including dimensions, materials, care instructions, and any customization options available.
- Anticipate potential questions or concerns that customers may have and address them proactively in your product descriptions.
- Be transparent about any limitations or drawbacks of your products to manage customer expectations effectively.

## 5. Use Keywords Strategically:

- Incorporate relevant keywords and phrases naturally into your product descriptions to improve search visibility.
- Focus on long-tail keywords that are specific to your products and have lower competition.
- Use variations of your keywords throughout your descriptions to cover a range of search queries.

## 6. Include Social Proof:

- Incorporate social proof into your product descriptions by highlighting positive reviews, testimonials, or endorsements from satisfied customers.
- Use phrases like "bestseller," "customer favorite," or "highly rated" to showcase the popularity and quality of your products.
- Encourage customers to leave reviews and feedback by offering incentives or reminders in your product descriptions.

**7. Create a Call to Action:**

- Conclude your product descriptions with a clear call to action that encourages customers to take the next step, such as "shop now," "add to cart," or "discover more."
- Use persuasive language to create a sense of urgency or excitement, such as "limited stock available" or "don't miss out on this exclusive offer."

**Conclusion:**

Enhancing your product listings with compelling descriptions is essential for attracting potential buyers and driving conversions in your Etsy shop. By highlighting key features and benefits, telling a story, using descriptive language, providing detailed information, using keywords strategically, incorporating social proof, and creating a call to action, you can create product descriptions that captivate customers and compel them to make a purchase. In the next chapter, we'll explore how to utilize social media to promote your print-on-demand products and reach a wider audience.

**Chapter 13: Utilizing Social Media to Promote Your Print-on-Demand Products**

Social media platforms offer powerful tools for promoting your print-on-demand products and reaching a broader audience of potential customers. In this chapter, we'll explore effective strategies for leveraging social media to increase visibility, drive traffic to your Etsy shop, and ultimately boost sales.

## 1. Choose the Right Platforms:

- Identify the social media platforms that are most relevant to your target audience and industry. Popular platforms for promoting print-on-demand products include Instagram, Facebook, Pinterest, and Twitter.
- Focus your efforts on platforms where your target audience is most active and engaged, and where visual content performs well.

## 2. Create Compelling Visual Content:

- Use high-quality images and graphics to showcase your print-on-demand products in a visually appealing way.
- Experiment with different types of content, such as product photos, lifestyle shots, behind-the-scenes glimpses, and user-generated content.
- Incorporate your branding elements, such as logos, colors, and fonts, to maintain a consistent look and feel across your social media profiles.

## 3. Engage with Your Audience:

- Foster meaningful interactions with your followers by responding to comments, messages, and mentions promptly.
- Encourage engagement by asking questions, running polls or contests, and soliciting user-generated content.
- Show appreciation for your followers by sharing user-generated content, featuring customer testimonials, and offering exclusive promotions or discounts.

## 4. Use Hashtags Strategically:

- Research relevant hashtags that are popular within your niche and use them strategically in your social media posts.
- Incorporate a mix of broad and specific hashtags to increase the visibility of your posts and attract a diverse audience.
- Create branded hashtags to encourage user-generated content and foster a sense of community around your brand.

## 5. Share Behind-the-Scenes Content:

- Give your followers a behind-the-scenes look at your print-on-demand business, including your creative process, production workflow, and team members.
- Humanize your brand by sharing stories, anecdotes, and personal experiences that resonate with your audience.
- Use Instagram Stories, Facebook Live, or other ephemeral content formats to provide real-time updates and exclusive sneak peeks.

## 6. Collaborate with Influencers and Partners:

- Identify influencers, bloggers, or other brands within your niche who have a significant following and engage with your target audience.
- Reach out to potential collaborators to explore partnership opportunities, such as sponsored posts, product reviews, or joint giveaways.
- Leverage the reach and credibility of influencers to amplify your brand message and introduce your print-on-demand products to a wider audience.

## 7. Analyze Performance and Adjust Your Strategy:

- Monitor the performance of your social media efforts using analytics tools provided by each platform.

- Track key metrics such as engagement rates, reach, click-through rates, and conversion rates to eva uate the effectiveness of your campaigns.
- Use insights from your analytics to identify what's working well and what can be improved, and adjust your social media strategy accordingly.

**Conclusion:**

Utilizing social media effectively can significantly enhance your efforts to promote your print-on-demand products and grow your Etsy shop. By choosing the right platforms, creating compelling visual content, engaging with your audience, using hashtags strategically, sharing behind-the-scenes content, collaborating with influencers and partners, and analyzing performance to adjust your strategy, you can leverage the power of social media to increase visibility, drive traffic, and ultimately boost sales. In the next chapter, we'll explore how to build an email list to expand your customer base and nurture relationships with your audience.

**Chapter 14: Building an Email List to Expand Your Customer Base**

Building an email list is a valuable strategy for expanding your customer base, nurturing relationships with your audience, and driving repeat sales for your print-on-demand products. In this chapter, we'll explore effective techniques for building an email list and leveraging it to grow your Etsy shop.

**1. Create Compelling Lead Magnets:**

- Offer valuable incentives, such as discounts, freebies, or exclusive content, in exchange for email sign-ups.
- Create compelling lead magnets that align with the interests and needs of your target audience, such as downloadable guides, e-books, or printable resources.

- Promote your lead magnets across your website, social media channels, and other marketing channels to attract potential subscribers.

## 2. Optimize Your Website and Etsy Shop for Sign-Ups:

- Place prominent opt-in forms and call-to-action buttons on your website and Etsy shop to encourage visitors to subscribe to your email list.
- Offer multiple opportunities for visitors to sign up throughout your site, such as in the header, footer, sidebar, and within blog posts or product pages.
- Use enticing copy and visuals to communicate the benefits of joining your email list and subscribing to your newsletter.

## 3. Utilize Pop-Up Forms and Exit-Intent Offers:

- Implement pop-up forms and exit-intent offers on your website and Etsy shop to capture visitors' attention and encourage them to subscribe.
- Use engaging headlines and compelling offers to entice visitors to sign up before they leave your site.
- Experiment with different timing and triggers for your pop-up forms to optimize their effectiveness without being intrusive.

## 4. Leverage Social Media and Content Marketing:

- Promote your email list on social media platforms by sharing links to sign-up forms and lead magnets in your posts and profiles.
- Create engaging content, such as blog posts, videos, or infographics, that provides value to your audience and encourages them to join your email list.
- Use social media advertising to target specific audience segments and drive traffic to your sign-up pages.

## 5. Host Giveaways and Contests:

- Host giveaways and contests on your website, social media channels, or other platforms to incentivize email sign-ups.
- Require participants to provide their email addresses as part of the entry process, and use a random selection tool to choose winners.
- Promote your giveaways and contests to your existing email list and social media followers to maximize participation and reach.

## 6. Personalize Your Email Content:

- Segment your email list based on factors such as demographics, purchase history, or engagement levels, and tailor your email content accordingly.
- Use personalized subject lines, greetings, and product recommendations to make your emails more relevant and engaging to subscribers.
- Experiment with dynamic content and automated email sequences to deliver targeted messages that resonate with different segments of your audience.

## 7. Provide Value and Nurture Relationships:

- Deliver valuable content to your email subscribers on a consistent basis, such as helpful tips, exclusive discounts, product updates, or behind-the-scenes insights.
- Nurture relationships with your subscribers by engaging with them directly through email, responding to their inquiries, and soliciting their feedback and opinions.
- Build trust and credibility with your audience over time by delivering on your promises, providing excellent customer service, and maintaining transparency and authenticity in your communications.

**Conclusion:**

Building an email list is a powerful strategy for expanding your customer base, increasing engagement, and driving sales for your print-on-demand products. By creating compelling lead magnets, optimizing your website and Etsy shop for sign-ups, utilizing pop-up forms and exit-intent offers, leveraging social media and content marketing, hosting giveaways and contests, personalizing your email content, and providing value and nurturing relationships with your subscribers, you can build a loyal and engaged audience that supports your Etsy shop and helps you achieve your business goals. In the next chapter, we'll explore strategies for providing excellent customer service and support to ensure a positive experience for your customers and subscribers.

**Chapter 15: Providing Excellent Customer Service and Support**

Providing excellent customer service and support is essential for building trust, fostering loyalty, and ensuring a positive experience for your customers and subscribers. In this chapter, we'll explore strategies for delivering exceptional customer service and support to enhance the reputation and success of your print-on-demand business.

**1. Offer Prompt and Responsive Communication:**

- Respond to customer inquiries, messages, and support requests promptly and professionally.
- Set clear expectations for response times and availability, and strive to exceed them whenever possible.
- Use multiple communication channels, such as email, social media, and live chat, to make it easy for customers to reach you and get the help they need.

**2. Listen to Your Customers' Needs and Feedback:**

- Take the time to listen to your customers' needs, concerns, and feedback, and make an effort to address them proactively.
- Encourage customers to share their opinions, suggestions, and experiences with your products and services, and use their feedback to make improvements.
- Show empathy and understanding when dealing with customer issues or complaints, and work collaboratively to find solutions that meet their needs.

### 3. Provide Clear and Transparent Information:

- Be transparent about your products, pricing, shipping policies, and any other relevant information to set clear expectations for your customers.
- Provide detailed product descriptions, sizing charts, and care instructions to help customers make informed purchasing decisions.
- Communicate openly and honestly about any delays, disruptions, or issues that may impact the customer experience, and provide regular updates as needed.

### 4. Go Above and Beyond to Exceed Expectations:

- Look for opportunities to surprise and delight your customers by going above and beyond their expectations.
- Offer personalized recommendations, customizations, or special touches to make each customer feel valued and appreciated.
- Anticipate potential needs or concerns and take proactive steps to address them before they become problems.

### 5. Resolve Issues and Complaints Promptly and Effectively:

- Take customer complaints and issues seriously, and make resolving them a top priority.

- Apologize sincerely for any mistakes or inconveniences, and take responsibility for finding a resolution that satisfies the customer.
- Offer refunds, replacements, or other solutions as appropriate to make things right and ensure customer satisfaction.

## 6. Empower Your Team to Deliver Exceptional Service:

- Provide comprehensive training and resources to your customer service team to equip them with the knowledge and skills they need to excel.
- Empower your team to make decisions and take action to resolve customer issues independently, without the need for constant supervision or approval.
- Foster a positive and supportive work environment that encourages teamwork, collaboration, and continuous improvement.

## 7. Solicit and Act on Customer Feedback:

- Regularly solicit feedback from your customers through surveys, reviews, and other feedback mechanisms.
- Analyze customer feedback systematically to identify patterns, trends, and areas for improvement.
- Use customer feedback to inform strategic decisions, prioritize improvements, and enhance the overall customer experience.

## Conclusion:

Providing excellent customer service and support is a cornerstone of success for any print-on-demand business. By offering prompt and responsive communication, listening to your customers' needs and feedback, providing clear and transparent information, going above and beyond to exceed expectations, resolving issues and complaints promptly and effectively, empowering your team to deliver exceptional service, and soliciting and acting on customer feedback, you can create a positive and memorable experience for your customers and subscribers that fosters loyalty and drives long-term success for your print-on-demand business. In the next chapter, we'll explore how to analyze your Etsy shop performance and track key metrics to measure success and identify areas for improvement.

### Chapter 16: Analyzing Your Etsy Shop Performance: Metrics to Track

Analyzing your Etsy shop's performance is crucial for understanding how your business is performing and identifying areas for improvement. In this chapter, we'll explore key metrics to track and analyze to measure the success of your print-on-demand business on Etsy.

### 1. Sales Performance Metrics:

- **Revenue:** Track your total revenue over a specific period to understand your shop's overall sales performance.
- **Sales Growth:** Monitor your sales growth rate to see how your revenue is trending over time and identify patterns or trends.
- **Average Order Value (AOV):** Calculate the average order value to understand how much customers are spending per transaction.

### 2. Traffic and Engagement Metrics:

- **Views:** Track the total number of views your shop and listings receive to measure overall visibility.

- **Visitors:** Monitor the number of unique visitors to your shop to understand how many individuals are interacting with your listings.
- **Conversion Rate:** Calculate the percentage of visitors who make a purchase to assess the effectiveness of your listings and marketing efforts.
- **Favorites and Engagement:** Keep track of the number of favorites, likes, shares, and comments on your listings to gauge customer interest and engagement.

### 3. Customer Behavior Metrics:

- **Repeat Customers:** Monitor the percentage of customers who make repeat purchases to measure customer loyalty and retention.
- **Customer Lifetime Value (CLV):** Calculate the average value of a customer over their entire relationship with your shop to assess long-term profitability.
- **Abandoned Cart Rate:** Track the percentage of visitors who add items to their cart but do not complete the purchase to identify potential barriers to conversion.

### 4. Listing Performance Metrics:

- **Bestselling Listings:** Identify your top-performing listings in terms of sales, views, and engagement to understand which products are resonating most with customers.
- **Conversion Rate by Listing:** Analyze the conversion rate for each listing to identify underperforming products and optimize their descriptions, pricing, or imagery.
- **Listing Quality Score:** Utilize Etsy's internal metrics, such as listing quality scores or search placement, to assess the effectiveness of your listings in Etsy's algorithm.

### 5. Marketing and Advertising Metrics:

- **Etsy Ads Performance:** Track the performance of your Etsy Ads campaigns, including click-through rates, cost per click, and return on ad spend (ROAS).
- **Social Media Referral Traffic:** Monitor the amount of traffic driven to your shop from social media platforms to evaluate the effectiveness of your social media marketing efforts.
- **Email Marketing Performance:** Measure the success of your email marketing campaigns, including open rates, click-through rates, and conversion rates, to assess the impact of your email list on sales.

## 6. Financial Metrics:

- **Profit Margin:** Calculate your profit margin for each product to ensure that your pricing strategy is generating sufficient profitability.
- **Expenses:** Track your operating expenses, including production costs, marketing expenses, and overhead, to understand your shop's overall financial health.
- **Return on Investment (ROI):** Evaluate the return on investment for your marketing efforts to assess the effectiveness of your advertising and promotional activities.

## 7. Customer Satisfaction Metrics:

- **Customer Reviews and Ratings:** Monitor customer reviews and ratings to gauge customer satisfaction and identify areas for improvement.
- **Response Time:** Measure your response time to customer inquiries and messages to ensure prompt and attentive customer service.

## Conclusion:

Analyzing your Etsy shop's performance is essential for optimizing your print-on-demand business and driving long-term success. By tracking and analyzing key metrics related to sales performance, traffic and engagement, customer behavior, listing performance, marketing and advertising, financials, and customer satisfaction, you can gain valuable insights into your shop's performance, identify areas for improvement, and make data-driven decisions to grow your business. In the next chapter, we'll explore strategies for scaling your print-on-demand business for growth and expansion.

**Chapter 17: Scaling Your Print-on-Demand Business for Growth**

Scaling your print-on-demand business is essential for expanding your reach, increasing sales, and achieving long-term success. In this chapter, we'll explore strategies for scaling your print-on-demand business effectively and efficiently.

**1. Automate and Streamline Processes:**

- Identify repetitive tasks and processes in your business operations, such as order processing, inventory management, and customer service, and look for opportunities to automate or streamline them.
- Invest in software tools and systems that can help automate routine tasks, such as order fulfillment platforms, inventory management software, and customer relationship management (CRM) systems.
- Streamline your production processes by working closely with reliable suppliers, optimizing production workflows, and implementing quality control measures to ensure consistency and efficiency.

**2. Expand Your Product Offering:**

- Diversify your product line by adding new products and designs to appeal to a broader audience and meet changing customer preferences.
- Conduct market research to identify potential product opportunities and trends within your niche, and develop new products that align with your brand and target audience.

- Experiment with different product categories, styes, and variations to see what resonates best with your customers anc drives the most sales.

### 3. Invest in Marketing and Advertising:

- Allocate resources to marketing and advertising efforts to increase visibility, attract new customers, and drive sales.
- Experiment with different marketing channels and strategies, such as social media advertising, search engine optimization (SEO), email marketing, influencer partnerships, and paid advertising, to reach your target audience effectively.
- Track and analyze the performance of your marketing campaigns to identify what's working well and where you can optimize your spending for maximum return on investment (ROI).

### 4. Build Brand Awareness and Loyalty:

- Invest in branding efforts to differentiate your print-on-demand business from competitors and build a strong brand identity that resonates with your target audience.
- Develop a consistent brand message and visual identity across all marketing channels and touchpoints, including your website, social media profiles, packaging, and customer communications.
- Foster a sense of community and connection with your customers by engaging with them regularly, soliciting feedback, and providing personalized experiences that demonstrate your commitment to their satisfaction and success.

### 5. Optimize Your Operations for Efficiency:

- Continuously evaluate and optimize your business operations to identify inefficiencies and bottlenecks that may be hindering growth.
- Streamline your supply chain and logistics processes to reduce lead times, minimize costs, and improve overall efficiency.
- Implement lean principles and practices, such as just-in-time inventory management, waste reduction, and continuous improvement, to increase productivity and profitability.

### 6. Focus on Customer Retention and Lifetime Value:

- Prioritize customer retention efforts to maximize the lifetime value of your customers and build a loyal customer base.
- Offer exceptional customer service and support, personalized recommendations, exclusive promotions, and rewards programs to incentivize repeat purchases and foster long-term relationships with your customers.
- Regularly engage with your customers through email marketing, social media, and other channels to stay top-of-mind and encourage ongoing engagement and loyalty.

**7. Monitor Key Performance Indicators (KPIs) and Adjust Your Strategy:**

- Track and analyze key performance indicators (KPIs) related to sales, revenue, profitability, customer acquisition, retention, and satisfaction to measure the success of your scaling efforts.
- Use data-driven insights to identify areas for improvement, adjust your strategy accordingly, and make informed decisions to drive continued growth and success.
- Stay agile and adaptable in your approach, and be willing to pivot or iterate on your strategy as needed to stay competitive and capitalize on emerging opportunities.

**Conclusion:**

Scaling your print-on-demand business for growth requires careful planning, strategic investments, and a relentless focus on delivering value to your customers. By automating and streamlining processes, expanding your product offering, investing in marketing and advertising, building brand awareness and loyalty, optimizing your operations for efficiency, focusing on customer retention and lifetime value, and monitoring key performance indicators (KPIs) to adjust your strategy, you can position your print-on-demand business for sustainable growth and long-term success. In the next chapter, we'll explore strategies for expanding your product line and offerings to diversify your revenue streams and reach new markets.

**Chapter 18: Expanding Your Product Line and Offerings**

Expanding your product line and offerings is a strategic approach to diversifying your revenue streams, attracting new customers, and maximizing the growth potential of your print-on-demand business. In this chapter, we'll explore effective strategies for expanding your product line and offerings to meet the evolving needs and preferences of your target audience.

## 1. Conduct Market Research:

Before expanding your product line, conduct thorough market research to identify gaps in the market, emerging trends, and opportunities for growth. Analyze customer feedback, industry trends, competitor offerings, and market demand to inform your product development strategy.

## 2. Diversify Product Categories:

Consider expanding into new product categories to broaden your appeal and reach new customer segments. Explore complementary products that align with your existing offerings and cater to the interests and preferences of your target audience. For example, if you currently sell apparel, consider adding accessories, home decor items, or stationery to your product line.

## 3. Introduce New Designs and Variations:

Keep your product offerings fresh and engaging by regularly introducing new designs, patterns, and variations. Experiment with different styles, themes, and color schemes to appeal to a diverse range of tastes and preferences. Leverage customer feedback and insights to guide your design decisions and identify which designs resonate most with your audience.

## 4. Offer Customization and Personalization Options:

Give customers the ability to customize and personalize their purchases to create unique and meaningful products. Offer options for personalized text, graphics, colors, and other design elements to allow customers to create one-of-a-kind items that reflect their individual style and personality. Consider implementing tools or features that simplify the custom zation process and make it easy for customers to create their own designs.

## 5. Collaborate with Artists and Designers:

Partner with independent artists, designers, and creators to expand your product line with unique and exclusive designs. Collaborate with artists whose style and aesthetic align with your brand to create co-branded collections or limited-edition collaborations that appeal to your target audience. Leverage the creativity and expertise of artists to introduce fresh and compelling designs that set your products apart from competitors.

### 6. Test New Products and Offerings:

Before fully committing to new products or offerings, conduct small-scale tests or pilot programs to gauge customer interest and validate demand. Launch limited-edition runs or exclusive previews to generate buzz and excitement around new products, and closely monitor customer feedback, sales performance, and market trends to inform future decisions.

### 7. Monitor Performance and Iterate:

Regularly monitor the performance of your expanded product line and offerings to identify what's working well and where there may be opportunities for improvement. Track key metrics such as sales, customer feedback, return rates, and profitability to assess the success of new products and iterations. Use insights from performance data to refine your product strategy, optimize your offerings, and prioritize future product development efforts.

### Conclusion:

Expanding your product line and offerings is a strategic approach to growing your print-on-demand business and maximizing your revenue potential. By conducting market research, diversifying product categories, introducing new designs and variations, offering customization and personalization options, collaborating with artists and designers, testing new products, and monitoring performance, you can attract new customers, enhance customer satisfaction, and drive long-term growth for your print-on-demand business. In the next chapter, we'll explore strategies for diversifying your sales channels beyond Etsy to reach new markets and expand your customer base.

## Chapter 19: Diversifying Your Sales Channels Beyond Etsy

Expanding beyond Etsy and diversifying your sales channels is a strategic move to reach new audiences, reduce reliance on a single platform, and grow your print-on-demand business. In this chapter, we'll explore effective strategies for diversifying your sales channels and expanding your reach beyond Etsy.

## 1. Launch Your Own E-commerce Website:

Create your own e-commerce website to establish a branded online presence and sell your print-on-demand products directly to customers. Choose a user-friendly platform, such as Shopify, WooCommerce, or BigCommerce, to build and customize your website, and integrate with print-on-demand fulfillment services to automate order processing and fulfillment.

## 2. Sell on Multiple Online Marketplaces:

Expand your reach by selling your print-on-demand products on multiple online marketplaces in addition to Etsy. Consider platforms such as Amazon, eBay, Walmart Marketplace, and Bonanza, which offer access to large and diverse customer bases. Optimize your product listings and pricing to maximize visibility and competitiveness across multiple marketplaces.

## 3. Explore Social Commerce Channels:

Leverage social media platforms as sales channels by setting up shop directly on social media platforms such as Facebook, Instagram, and Pinterest. Use features like Facebook Shops, Instagram Shopping, and Pinterest Buyable Pins to showcase your products, tag them in posts and stories, and facilitate seamless transactions directly within the social media platform.

## 4. Partner with Retailers and Resellers:

Explore partnerships with brick-and-mortar retailers, online retailers, and resellers to expand your distribution channels and reach new markets. Collaborate with retailers that cater to your target audience or niche market and negotiate wholesale or consignment agreements to sell your print-on-demand products through their channels.

### 5. Attend Trade Shows and Events:

Participate in trade shows, craft fairs, pop-up markets, and other events to showcase your print-on-demand products and connect with potential customers in person. Research relevant events within your industry or niche, and create eye-catching displays and promotional materials to attract attendees and generate sales leads.

### 6. Explore Wholesale and B2B Opportunities:

Explore opportunities to sell your print-on-demand products wholesale or to business-to-business (B2B) customers, such as retailers, corporate clients, event planners, and organizations. Develop wholesale pricing structures, catalogs, and sales materials to pitch your products to potential wholesale and B2B customers and expand your distribution channels.

### 7. Build a Network of Affiliates and Influencers:

Build relationships with affiliates, influencers, bloggers, and content creators within your niche to promote your print-on-demand products to their audience. Offer affiliate commissions, sponsorships, or free products in exchange for promotion and referrals, and track affiliate performance to optimize your partnership strategies.

### Conclusion:

Diversifying your sales channels beyond Etsy is a strategic approach to expanding your reach, increasing sales, and growing your print-on-demand business. By launching your own e-commerce website, selling on multiple online marketplaces, exploring social commerce channels, partnering with retailers and resellers, attending trade shows and events, exploring wholesale and B2B opportunities, and building a network of affiliates and influencers, you can reach new audiences, reduce dependency on a single platform, and unlock new growth opportunities for your print-on-demand business. In the next chapter, we'll conclude our guide and provide actionable steps for taking your print-on-demand business to the next level.

## Conclusion: Taking Your Print-on-Demand Store to the Next Level

Congratulations on completing this comprehensive guide to building and growing a profitable print-on-demand store with Etsy and Printify. By following the strategies and techniques outlined in this guide, you've gained valuable insights into the print-on-demand business model, learned how to leverage platforms like Etsy and Printify, and discovered effective strategies for setting up, scaling, and diversifying your print-on-demand business.

As you embark on the next phase of your print-on-demand journey, here are some key takeaways to keep in mind:

**1. Focus on Quality and Customer Satisfaction:** Always prioritize quality and customer satisfaction in everything you do. Delivering high-quality products and exceptional customer service is crucial for building trust, fostering loyalty, and driving repeat business.

**2. Stay Agile and Adaptable:** The print-on-demand landscape is constantly evolving, so it's important to stay agile and adaptable in your approach. Keep an eye on market trends, customer preferences, and emerging technologies, and be willing to pivot or iterate on your strategy as needed to stay competitive and capitalize on new opportunities.

**3. Continuously Improve and Innovate:** Never stop learning and growing. Continuously seek opportunities to improve your products, processes, and customer experience. Experiment with new ideas, test different strategies, and learn from both successes and failures to refine your approach and drive continuous innovation.

**4. Build and Nurture Relationships:** Cultivate strong relationships with your customers, suppliers, partners, and community. Engage with your audience regularly, listen to their feedback, and show genuine appreciation for their support. Building a loyal and engaged customer base is key to long-term success in the print-on-demand business.

**5. Measure Success and Track Progress:** Set clear goals and metrics to measure the success of your print-on-demand business. Track key performance indicators (KPIs) such as sales, revenue, customer satisfaction, and profitability, and use data-driven insights to make informed decisions and drive growth.

**6. Take Risks and Embrace Challenges:** Building and growing a print-on-demand business is not without its challenges, but don't be afraid to take risks and embrace new opportunities. Be willing to step out of your comfort zone, try new things, and push the boundaries of what's possible. It's through taking risks and overcoming challenges that you'll truly unlock your full potential.

**7. Stay Passionate and Persistent:** Above all, stay passionate and persistent in pursuit of your goals. Building a successful print-on-demand business takes time, effort, and dedication, but with passion, perseverance, and a positive mindset, you can overcome any obstacle and achieve your dreams.

As you continue your print-on-demand journey, remember that success is not just about reaching a destination—it's about enjoying the journey, embracing the ups and downs, and celebrating every milestone along the way. Keep learning, keep growing, and keep pushing yourself to new heights. With determination, creativity, and a commitment to excellence, there's no limit to what you can achieve with your print-on-demand store.

Thank you for joining us on this journey, and we wish you all the best in your future endeavors. Here's to taking your print-on-demand store to the next level!

Sincerely,

Virginia Green, Author